The Western Front

Nicola Barber

HODDER
Wayland

an imprint of Hodder Children's Books

© 2003 White-Thomson Publishing Ltd

Produced for Hodder Wayland by
White-Thomson Publishing Ltd
2/3 St Andrew's Place
Lewes BN7 1UP

Other titles in this series:
The African-American Slave Trade
The Causes of World War II
The Cold War
The Holocaust

Editor: Anna Lee
Designer: Derek Lee
Consultant: Neil DeMarco
Proofreader: Philippa Smith
Picture research: Shelley Noronha, Glass Onion
Pictures
Maps: The Map Studio

Published in Great Britain in 2003 by Hodder
Wayland, an imprint of Hodder Children's Books.

British Library Cataloguing in Publication Data
Barber, Nicola
    The Western Front. - (Questioning history)
    1.World War, 1914-1918 - Campaigns -
    Western Front -
    Juvenile literature
    I.Title II.Lee, Anna
    940.4'144

ISBN 07502 4081 4

Printed in Hong Kong, China

Hodder Children's Books
A division of Hodder Headline Limited
338 Euston Road, London NW1 3BH

Picture acknowledgements:
AKG 8, 17, 18, 22, 23, 24, 26, 31, 36, 38, 48, 57,
59; Camera Press 21, 33; Hodder Wayland Picture
Library 10, 30, 32, 43, 58; Mary Evans 44, 49, 50;
Peter Newark Military Pictures 35, 54;
Popperphoto 6, 7, 15, 20, 28, 34, 42, 46, 52, 56;
Topham 13, 29, 39, 41.

Cover Picture: A wounded British soldier is
brought to safety after the Battle of the Ancre
in November 1916 - the closing stages of the
Somme campaign.

CONTENTS

CHAPTER 1

Going to War

ALLIANCES

When war broke out in 1914, a system of alliances between different countries ensured that the conflict quickly involved most of the major European powers. By 1914, the two main groupings were the Triple Alliance between Germany, Austria-Hungary and Italy, and the Triple Entente between Britain, France and Russia. But these alliances had their origins in events over 40 years earlier.

In 1871, Prussia (a north German state) defeated France in the Franco-Prussian War. The end of the Franco-Prussian War also marked the unification of the separate German states into a single power, the German Empire. The war served to heighten tensions between France and its neighbour, but many other European states also began to look with some alarm at the new power in the centre of Europe.

BELOW *Europe in 1914.*

Central Powers 1914
Neutral countries later aligned with Central Powers
Allies 1914
Neutral countries later aligned with Allies
Allied with Central Powers, declared neutrality at outbreak of war, then joined Allies
Countries remaining neutral

FINLAND
NORWAY
St Petersburg
Christiania
SWEDEN
Stockholm
Moscow
RUSSIAN EMPIRE
Edinburgh
DENMARK
Copenhagen
Dublin
NETHERLANDS
GREAT BRITAIN
London
Amsterdam
Berlin
POLAND
Brussels
GERMANY
BELGIUM
ATLANTIC OCEAN
Paris
LUXEMBOURG
Vienna
SWITZERLAND
FRANCE
Berne
AUSTRIA-HUNGARY
ROMANIA
Bucharest
BLACK SEA
BOSNIA
SERBIA
BULGARIA
ITALY
MONTENEGRO
Sofia
Constantinople
PORTUGAL
Madrid
Corsica
Rome
ALBANIA
OTTOMAN EMPIRE (TURKEY)
Lisbon
SPAIN
Sardinia
GREECE
MEDITERRANEAN
Sicily
Athens
SEA
Cyprus

0 — 500 miles
0 — 500 kilometres

Otto von Bismarck, the first chancellor of Germany, negotiated an alliance with Austria-Hungary in 1879 (the Dual Alliance), and in 1882 with Austria-Hungary and Italy (the Triple Alliance). These agreements were based on defence – countries promised to come to each other's aid if they were attacked. Prompted by fear of the power of the Triple Alliance, Russia and France made their own defensive alliance in 1894. Germany now found itself with powerful potential enemies on both sides.

Britain remained aloof throughout the nineteenth century, secure in prosperity gained from its industrial might and its vast empire. But by the beginning of the twentieth century the situation was beginning to look rather different. Other countries, including Germany, were starting to rival Britain's industrial ouput. The difficulties and high death toll of the Boer Wars (1899-1902) in South Africa also weakened Britain's once unshakeable confidence. In 1904, Britain entered into an agreement with France, known as the Entente Cordiale. This was not a defensive agreement, in fact it dealt mainly with colonial matters, but it was nevertheless viewed as a military threat by Germany. A similar agreement was made with Russia in 1907, and soon people began to use the term 'Triple Entente' to describe the alliance between Britain, France and Russia.

? EVENT IN QUESTION

Did the alliance system help to start the war?

At first, defensive agreements were intended to reduce the possibility of one country declaring war on another from the opposing alliance. But some historians have argued that the alliances helped to turn a small, local quarrel into a major conflict. It is probably true that the alliances helped to provoke mistrust between the opposing European powers, and Germany certainly made war plans as a direct result of the perceived threat of the 1894 Franco-Russian agreement (see above). However, when matters came to a head in 1914, countries acted in their own national interests, often despite the terms of the alliances. For example, Italy refused to back its partners in the Triple Alliance, and Britain went to war in support of France although not obliged to under the terms of the Triple Entente.

THE RACE TO ARMS

Throughout the nineteenth century Britain had taken for granted the superiority of its navy over that of any other country. Then in 1897, Admiral Alfred von Tirpitz, German State Secretary for the Navy, decided to begin building a German high seas fleet to rival the British fleet. Tirpitz's aim was to construct a navy so powerful that it would threaten Britain's dominance of the seas and act as a deterrent to any confrontation. However, the British responded by increasing the rate of production of ships for their own fleet and in 1906 introduced the Dreadnought, a new type of battleship. Despite the costs of this naval arms race, Britain refused to give up its naval dominance because it considered the threat from Germany to be too great. When war broke out in 1914 Germany had 17 large warships and Britain had 29.

Hand-in-hand with the building of battleships went the construction of new docks, and in Germany the widening of the Kiel Canal to allow even the largest battleships to sail between the Baltic Sea and the North Sea. There was also an acceleration in the production of other armaments. The Industrial Revolution, which started in Britain in the late eighteenth century, had a major impact on the manufacture of arms. Instead of being made individually by hand, from the 1840s onwards, guns and other weapons could be mass-produced in factories. Companies such as Krupps in Germany and Vickers in Britain became booming businesses – by 1914 the Krupps factories at Essen were Germany's biggest industrial works.

BELOW *The might of the British navy on show at Spithead.*

EXPANDING THE MILITARY

Most European countries also built up large armed forces in readiness for a potential war. The exception was Britain, which had no history of compulsory military service. In Germany, the armed forces commanded huge respect and the peacetime army was made up of 700,000 trained soldiers. Furthermore, the German commanders knew that if and when they decided to mobilize they could call on thousands more reservists to be ready within a week.

ABOVE *The armaments business: women fill shells with shrapnel at the Krupps factory in Essen, Germany.*

? EVENT IN QUESTION

Did the arms race contribute to the outbreak of war?

The naval arms race caused a great deal of antagonism between Germany and Britain. Propaganda reports in the press helped to stir up suspicion, preparing the ground for a possible conflict. Sir Edward Grey, British Foreign Secretary, wrote in 1925, 'The enormous growth of armaments in Europe, the sense of insecurity and fear caused by them – it was these that made the war inevitable…' Whether he was correct in his view has been questioned by many historians. Although Britain spent most on armaments in the pre-war years it least wanted war. Germany spent less on defence than Britain, and yet it was deeply concerned about threats from Russia and France. It seems that the arms race was only one of many interlinked factors that tipped Europe from a fragile peace into all-out war.

TIPPING THE BALANCE

The event that tipped the balance towards war took place in Sarajevo in June 1914. Sarajevo was the capital of Bosnia-Herzegovina, a Balkan state that had been under the administration of Austria-Hungary since 1878, and was annexed (taken over) by Austria-Hungary in 1908. The population of Bosnia-Herzegovina included Serbs of Slavic origin who were deeply opposed to Austria-Hungary's rule. They were supported by many people in neighbouring Serbia who believed that there should be a separate Slav state in the Balkans. Austria-Hungary wanted to increase its influence in the Balkans and regarded Serbia as a serious nuisance. Russia also supported its southern Slavic relations, and had been prepared to mobilize troops in support of Serbia in the Balkan War of 1912-13. It was against this background of political turmoil that Archduke Franz Ferdinand, heir to the throne of Austria-Hungary, decided to visit Sarajevo in 1914.

Austrian diplomats advised the Archduke not to make the visit, especially as the date on which it was to occur was Vivdovan,

BELOW *The Archduke Franz Ferdinand and his wife Sophie with their entourage in Sarajevo on 28 June 1914. The events of this day ignited the First World War.*

the most important Serbian national festival of the year. But the Archduke refused to listen to the warnings and on 28 June he and his wife Sophie arrived in Sarajevo. The couple were driven around the streets of the city in an open-topped car. At one point a bomb was thrown at the car, but it bounced off and exploded behind the royal couple, leaving them unhurt. Then their car took a wrong turning and as it slowed, shots rang out. Both the Archduke and his wife were killed by Gavrilo Princip, a member of a Bosnian Serb nationalist group called the Black Hand Gang.

In Austria-Hungary the news was greeted with outrage. The government decided to use the killings as an excuse to end Serbian influence in the Balkans, blaming the Serbian govern-ment for the assassination. Austria-Hungary knew it could rely on Germany's backing in the event of a war with Serbia; it also knew that going to war with Serbia might provoke Russian inter-vention and therefore provoke a Europe-wide war. Nevertheless, on 23 July Austria-Hungary issued an ultimatum to Serbia that was made up of ten demands designed to curb Serb nationalists. On Russia's advice, Serbia agreed to all of these demands with the exception of one, but Austria-Hungary refused to agree to any-thing but complete acceptance of the ultimatum. Five days later, on 28 July, Austria-Hungary declared war on Serbia.

? WHAT IF...

The Archduke Franz Ferdinand had listened to the advice not to visit Sarajevo?

We have seen that the conditions for war were already present in Europe in 1914. Two opposing blocs of alliances, the arms race and the build-up of military power all led to a climate of fear and suspicion. Some historians think that both Austria-Hungary and Germany were looking for an excuse for war: Austria-Hungary wanted to settle its claims in the Balkans, and Germany was feeling increasingly under threat from its powerful neighbours France and Russia. However, most people assumed that any war that did break out would be a short one. The death of the Archduke provided the spark that lit the fuse of war, but it is likely that if he had visited Sarajevo on another day and survived, another excuse to start a conflict would have cropped up somewhere else.

ABOVE *War is declared in Germany: the official announcement is read out to a packed crowd.*

DECLARING WAR

It is possible that the decision-makers in the government of Austria-Hungary thought they would be able to make a quick strike on Serbia and achieve their aims before Russia could act. But they were wrong. Russia mobilized its army on 30 July, two days after Austria-Hungary's declaration of war, although it still expressed a strong desire for a negotiated settlement. In response Germany issued an ultimatum to Russia to stop its military preparations, and when Russia declined Germany declared war on Russia on 1 August. This brought the German Schlieffen Plan (see page 12) into immediate action, and the next day Germany asked Belgium for safe passage for its troops on their way to attack France. Belgium refused, Germany declared war on France on 3 August, and German troops invaded Belgium the following day.

Up until this point, Britain had been on the sidelines, although Sir Edward Grey had made efforts to solve the crisis through diplomacy. The British government refused to give a direct commitment to support France if it was attacked by Germany, but it was the issue of Belgian neutrality that eventually drew Britain into the conflict. From 1839 there had been an international agreement to maintain Belgian neutrality, so when Germany violated this agreement, Britain was obliged to respond. Britain declared war on Germany on 4 August, and the first British troops were sent to France soon after.

THE AMERICAN RESPONSE

Across the Atlantic Ocean people in the USA greeted the news of war in Europe with shock, but few thought that America would become involved. In 1914 America took a neutral stance, favouring neither the Allies (France, Russia and Britain) nor the Central Powers (Germany and Austria-Hungary). In theory, American companies were free to export armaments and supplies to countries on either side of the conflict. However, Britain used its superior naval forces to blockade the Central Powers and prevent supplies coming through. This meant that American trade with Germany declined while trade with Britain and France increased. In 1915 Germany responded to the blockade by using its fleet of submarines (called U-boats) to blockade British waters. Disaster struck when a German U-boat attacked and sank a British passenger ship, the *Lusitania*, on 7 May 1915. Over one thousand people were drowned, including 128 American citizens. The incident provoked outrage in the USA, and marked a turning-point in American attitudes. However, it was another two years before the USA entered the war (see page 29).

? WHAT IF...

Britain had stayed out of the war?

If Britain had not declared war on 4 August 1914, British troops would not have gone to France two days later. It seems most likely that Germany would have overcome French resistance. There would have been no Battle of the Marne (see page 14) and no Western Front. The war may not have become a world war, nor would the United States have become involved. In his book *The Pity of War*, the historian Niall Ferguson suggests that a rapid German victory would have eventually resulted in the transformation of Europe into something like 'the European Union we know today...' but without the two world wars of the twentieth century. He goes on to call the First World War the 'greatest error of modern history'.

CHAPTER 2

Scenes of Battle

THE SCHLIEFFEN PLAN

When France and Russia entered into a formal alliance in 1894, Germany's response was to draw up a military plan for possible future war. The 'Schlieffen Plan' was named after the German Chief of General Staff Alfred von Schlieffen.

The Schlieffen Plan aimed to avoid fighting a war on two fronts at the same time: a rapid victory against France in the west was planned before moving east to crush Russia. The border between Germany and France was heavily fortified on the French side, so Schlieffen decided the attack on France would take place further west, by sending the right wing of a huge army through Belgium and then turning westwards to Paris. A left wing would attack France through Alsace-Lorraine. The planned outcome was that the French army would be squeezed and trapped between the two wings. The plan depended upon railways to move troops and equipment efficiently to the German border. It also depended on speed.

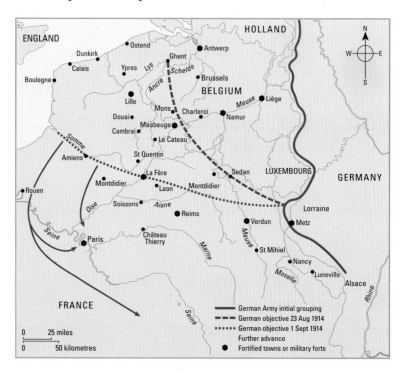

RIGHT *The Schlieffen Plan.*

ABOVE *Soldiers from the Belgian army prepare to defend a road against German troops in 1914.*

Schlieffen retired in 1906 and his place was taken by Helmuth von Moltke, who eventually put the plan into action. The demands of the Schlieffen Plan meant that as soon as Russia started to mobilize its troops in July 1914, Germany had to move quickly against France. German troops invaded Belgium on 4 August; by 20 August they had captured Brussels. They encountered more resistance than expected from the Belgians, but it was not enough to hold them back. Meanwhile, the British Expeditionary Force (BEF) (see page 14) had landed in northern France and made its way towards the fighting. The first battle to involve the BEF was at Mons, but although it halted the Germans for several days it was indecisive. The French army and the BEF began to retreat south-wards. However, on 26 August Moltke diverted many troops from the right wing in Belgium to East Prussia, where there was trouble with the Russians. The Germans now lacked sufficient troops to encircle Paris, and the Schlieffen Plan began to unravel.

? EVENT IN QUESTION

What was wrong with Schlieffen's plan?

Even before war was declared there were concerns about the Schlieffen Plan. Could sufficient German troops move rapidly enough to overwhelm the French forces without becoming exhausted, or running out of supplies? Would Russia mobilize more quickly than the Germans thought they could? When Moltke took over from Schlieffen he increased the size of the German army, but was unable to resolve the problems of movement and supply. In the event, German troops often marched until they were exhausted, frequently going without food because supplies could not keep up. The plan also started to fail as it was adapted on the ground. Moltke weakened the right wing by removing troops to go to East Prussia, and German general, Alexander von Kluck, moved the army under his command south-east towards Paris, rather than in the westwards pincer movement specified in the Schlieffen Plan.

THE ALLIES ATTACK

Although the Schlieffen Plan was proving unworkable, German troops were within 48 kilometres of Paris by the beginning of September 1914. The city emptied as residents fled, and the French government moved to Bordeaux. Moving in the opposite direction, French reservists hurried to the front line travelling by any means possible – including 600 taxis commandeered by the military. Moltke sensed victory, but the German troops had marched continuously for 33 days and the men were exhausted. When the French and British began to attack along the River Marne, the Germans were unable to resist. The Battle of the Marne was inconclusive, but it prevented the Germans from marching into Paris. On 9 September, Moltke gave the order for the German armies to retreat to safer defensive positions north of the Marne. The Schlieffen Plan was finally at an end.

The German armies retreated to the River Aisne, where they set about preparing defensive fortifications on high ground north of the river – the first trenches of the war. Moltke had failed, and he was replaced by General Erich von Falkenhayn.

THE RACE TO THE SEA

The Allies attempted several attacks on the Aisne but found the German positions too strong. What followed was a series of attacks to the north of the Aisne, as both sides tried to establish superiority in the area of land between the Aisne and the sea. This is often called the 'Race to the Sea', as the Germans tried to cut off the BEF from the Channel ports and a means of retreat. The culmination of these manouevres was the First Battle of Ypres in October 1914, when the British force, with vital reinforcements from Indian units, managed to hold the line. It was at a great cost, however: the original BEF was almost wiped out, and thousands of young German student volunteers died in the fighting.

STALEMATE

As the First Battle of Ypres drew to a close, and winter started to set in, neither side was in a position to launch a new offensive. Both the Germans and the Allies dug themselves into defensive trenches that now stretched in a line over 540 kilometres long, from the North Sea to Switzerland. In four months, the war had gone from one of rapid movement to complete stalemate. Both sides were exhausted, short of munitions, and shocked by the already huge losses. It was the beginning of the war of attrition.

ABOVE *The British Expeditionary Force (BEF) in Ypres in October 1914. By the end of the war, the town of Ypres was completely devastated.*

? WHAT IF...

The Germans had captured Paris?

If the Germans had been able to continue the momentum of their great march southwards another 48 kilometres to Paris, the story of the First World War would have been very different. There would have been no 'Race to the Sea' and no First Battle of Ypres. In all probability the BEF would have returned home largely unscathed. The Germans would have taken control of the channel ports, straining relations with Britain, but it is likely that Britain's involvement in the war would have been at an end. Parts of France would have been taken over by Germany, fuelling even more antagonism between the two countries. But with no Western Front, millions of lives would have been saved.

ATTACK OR DEFENCE?

In August 1914 it was Germany who had attacked, across Belgium and into northern France. But as stalemate set in after the First Battle of Ypres the Germans adopted a different strategy. Instructed by Moltke in September 1914 to 'entrench and hold' the positions reached after the Battle of the Marne, they constructed deep, strongly fortified trench systems that became increasingly sophisticated as the war progressed. The Germans also hoped to keep things relatively quiet on the Western Front because of their need to move troops to the east, where, in January 1915, reinforcements were needed to fight the Russians.

The Allies, meanwhile, were more interested in a strategy of attack. For the French it was a matter of national economics and pride. The areas captured by the Germans were largely industrial regions of France, and it was unthinkable for the French commander, Marshal Joseph Joffre, that his troops should spend time

BELOW *The Western Front.*

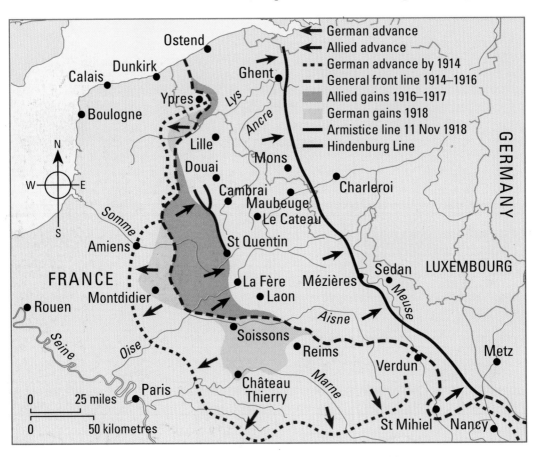

and effort building a strong defensive line because his policy was to be one of attack and recovery of the captured land.

The British command put its faith in an ability to wear the enemy down by inflicting more casualties on the Germans than the Germans could inflict on the Allies – a war of attrition. The reasoning behind such attacks as the Battle of the Somme was 'to kill as many Germans as possible with the least loss to ourselves'.

On 16 March 1917 the Germans once again used a defensive tactic to strengthen their position on the Western Front. They began Operation Alberich to withdraw from certain sections of the Western Front to a previously prepared and heavily fortified defensive line about 30 kilometres behind their old positions. The withdrawal shortened the German front line, making it easier to defend, and freed up yet more troops to be sent to the east. The new line was known to the Germans as the Siegfried Line, and to the Allies as the Hindenburg Line after the German commander, Field Marshal Paul von Hindenburg.

BELOW *German troops in a trench in 1914. Many German trenches were deep and well-constructed, as shown here.*

? EVENT IN QUESTION

What new defensive tactics were introduced by the Germans?

As the war continued the Germans refined their tactics of defence. Along the Hindenburg Line a system of defensive lines, up to 7.3 kilometres deep, was created so that attacking troops would become exhausted before they could penetrate beyond the final line of defence. Another innovation was to dig front lines on the far side of hills, rather than on the facing slope to the enemy. This meant that troops were hidden from the opposing enemy lines. In the event of an attack, warning was given by the lookouts and by the machine gunners. The enemy could then be attacked as they appeared over the crest of the hill.

VERDUN 1916

By the end of 1915, French casualties numbered over 200,000, half of them dead. The German commander General Erich von Falkenhayn decided to launch an offensive in early 1916 to lure the French army into combat, and to inflict more damage on the French forces. He chose the area of front line around the fortress of Verdun as the site for his offensive. Falkenhayn guessed that French pride would not allow Verdun to be given up easily, and he calculated that for every German killed in the attack, three French soldiers would die.

What Falkenhayn did not know was that despite its formidable fortifications Verdun and its surrounding forts had mostly been stripped of guns and troops. The French had watched the ease with which the Belgian fortresses of Liège and Namur had

BELOW *A deserted trench surrounded by deep mud and corpses at Fort Douaumont, during the Battle of Verdun.*

fallen to the Germans in 1914, and had decided that such fortifications were ineffective against heavy German guns. So when operation Gericht ('judgement') was launched in February the French were largely unprepared. The Germans quickly made progress, taking the major stronghold of Fort Douaumont. Falkenhayn began to worry that Verdun would fall too easily without the war of attrition he had planned. But as the situation became critical, the French command decided that Verdun was to be defended as a matter of honour – just as Falkenhayn had hoped.

General Pétain was put in charge of French operations at Verdun, and soon reinforcements were arriving along the only supply route into the fort on the French side, known as 'la voie sacrée' ('the sacred way'). The fighting dragged on for months as the two sides attacked and counter-attacked. Both the Germans and the French sustained heavy casualties, proving Falkenhayn's gruesome calculation wrong. At the beginning of May, General Robert Nivelle took over command of the French troops from Pétain. After a particularly intensive German barrage in June he strengthened the resolve of his troops with the words 'On ne passe pas!' (They shall not pass!).

The turning point of the battle for Verdun came in June. Just as in 1914, the German high command was forced to withdraw some troops from the Western Front at Verdun to send to the east, where the Russians had launched a new offensive. Soon after, the British forces attacked on the Somme (see page 21). As the autumn came, the French began to regain territory, making use of new tactics such as the creeping barrage (see page 37) introduced by Nivelle. But it was not until August 1917 that the French recovered their front line positions of February 1916.

? WHAT IF...

The French had decided not to defend Verdun?

Despite a reputation as a tenacious defender, Pétain had his doubts about the wisdom of defending Verdun. In March 1917, he suggested to the French president, Raymond Poincaré, the possibility of withdrawing from the fort and allowing the Germans to take it. The answer came back: 'Don't think of it General. It would be a parliamentary catastrophe.' And so the fate of one-and-a-half million soldiers was sealed. If the French had chosen not to defend, or if the Germans had been able to press their advantage and take the fort, it is possible that the war would have ended far sooner, as France may have accepted some kind of compromise agreement with Germany.

THE SOMME 1916

Early in 1916, the Allies began to plan a joint attack against the German front line in the area of the Somme. The new British commander, Douglas Haig, would have preferred to mount an offensive around Ypres, but conceded to the insistence of the French commander Marshal Joseph Joffre that the attack should be where British and French forces met. Haig hoped to make a breakthrough on the Somme and push the Germans back. Joffre's aim was one of attrition – to kill as many Germans as possible.

The timing of the Somme attack was affected by events at Verdun (see pages 18-19). As the Germans made advances at Verdun, Joffre and Pétain appealed to Haig for the Somme offensive to start as soon as possible to relieve their forces. Reluctantly Haig agreed that the attack should start some weeks earlier than originally planned, on 1 July 1916. As fewer French troops were available for the Somme offensive, it was agreed that British troops would play the major role. Many of these troops were volunteers, part of 'Kitchener's Army'. They were joined by forces from Australia, Canada, India, New Zealand and South Africa.

? PEOPLE IN QUESTION

General Sir Douglas Haig (1861–1928)

In accounts of the Battle of the Somme, Haig was greatly criticized. He was suspicious of those junior to him, and unwilling to listen to advice. He was convinced that only a major attack on the Western Front would finally bring the war to an end. So when British patrols brought news that the preliminary bombardment had had little effect on the German wire or front lines, Haig's second-in-command failed to pass this information on – he knew Haig did not respond well to criticism. On 30 June, Haig noted in his diary that the wire 'had never been so well cut, nor the artillery preparation so thorough…'

Many of Kitchener's volunteer army were only half-trained, and few had any experience of battle. Haig ordered a massive artillery bombardment of the German front line which started on 24 June. The idea was that the shelling would empty the German front lines and rip holes in the barbed wire in No Man's Land (see page 32). In fact, the Germans had built deep protective dugouts in the Somme where they retreated during the shelling. The shells also proved ineffective against the wire.

On 1 July the Allied attack began. The plan was that waves of Allied troops would walk out of their front lines, through the gaps created in the German barbed wire and into the empty German front lines. However, the Germans set up their machine guns and shot down the attacking troops. It was the worst day in British military history: about 60,000 casualties, 20,000 of whom died. Yet the battle continued until 19 November. Allied casualties amounted to 600,000 men; they gained about 11 kilometres of territory.

ABOVE *A wounded British soldier is carried to safety during one of the battles of the Somme offensive in 1916. Heavy autumn rains had turned the battlefield into a sea of deep, stinking mud.*

Robert Nivelle (1857–1924)

How did Nivelle manage to convince people that his attack should go ahead, and what made him so sure that it would be successful? Nivelle was charming, handsome and very confident. He spoke perfect English, and quickly won round the British Prime Minister, David Lloyd George, who preferred to trust the French general rather than Douglas Haig. When Nivelle met resistance to his plans from his own government he threatened to resign, which quickly silenced all opposition. Fresh from the recapture of Verdun, Nivelle was keen to use the same tactics again. However, Nivelle took no account of the fact that his troops would be attacking a well-prepared and strongly held defensive line, and Nivelle's attack was a failure.

THE NIVELLE OFFENSIVE

In December 1916, after the failure of the Somme campaign and the fighting at Verdun, the French general Robert Nivelle replaced Joffre as commander of French troops on the Western Front. Nivelle had been responsible for the French recapture of Verdun, and he now wanted to build on this success. In January 1917 he explained his plans for a new attack to the British government.

The British commander General Sir Douglas Haig had planned to continue attacking the German front line on the Somme in 1917, but Nivelle wanted to concentrate a powerful attack in the Champagne region, to the east of the Somme, as well as a diversionary attack to the west of the Somme, around Arras. Nivelle declared: 'We shall break the German front when we wish, provided we do not attack the strongest point and that we execute the operation by surprise and abrupt attack, in 24 hours or 48 hours.' Nivelle's plan was that the two attacks should 'squeeze' the westwards bulge (known as a salient) in the German front line and eliminate it.

In fact, it did not require any fighting to eliminate the salient because in March 1917 the Germans themselves withdrew to the formidable defences of the Hindenburg Line (see page 17), destroying everything in their path as they retreated. Nevertheless Nivelle was determined to continue with his planned offensive. Despite opposition to his plans in the French government, Nivelle finally convinced enough people that his offensive would bring about the end of the fighting on the Western Front.

The Battle of Arras started on 9 April and at first appeared to be a success as Canadian troops stormed on to Vimy Ridge. But the Allied commanders failed to take advantage of their troops' initial success, and by the time orders came for the attack the Germans had had time to regroup. The French attacked in the Champagne region on 16 April, along a part of the front line known as the 'Chemin des Dames'. But the Germans had plenty of warning of this attack, and had been digging fortifications in this part of the line for over two years. The attack continued for weeks but eventually failed. The French suffered over 100,000 casualties and mutinies broke out in the army (see page 53). On 15 May Nivelle was replaced as commander of the French forces by General Henri Pétain.

BELOW *French army cooks prepare food for the troops in the area of the front line known as the Chemin des Dames.*

ABOVE *This is the scene of devastation on the battlefield near Passchendaele after the battles of July and August 1917. The offensive continued for another three months, and many thousands of soldiers died in the mud.*

THIRD YPRES / PASSCHENDAELE 1917

In 1917, Haig finally succeeded in his desire to launch an attack in the area around Ypres. The French army was still recovering from the mutinies that had followed the Nivelle Offensive, so the initiative passed to the British. Haig's aim was to break through the German defences at Ypres and retake Belgium, capturing the seaports of Zeebrugge and Ostende from where it was believed German U-boats were operating. Prime Minister Lloyd George was unwilling to allow the attack – he feared a repeat of the terrible slaughter of the Somme. But he was finally argued down by Haig and his advisers.

Haig's belief in the soundness of his plan was boosted by the capture of Messines Ridge in June 1917. This ridge formed the southern part of the Ypres salient, and it was vital for it to be taken before the attack on Ypres could start. The British dug 8 kilometres of tunnels beneath the ridge and packed them with high explosive. When the mines were detonated on 7 June the blast was heard in London. However, the capture of the ridge was followed by a lull of seven weeks as the British prepared for the major offensive. Once again, the British were attacking deep, well-prepared German defences; once again, as at the Somme, Haig planned a massive preliminary bombardment to pulverize the German defences. The bombardment started on 17 July and lasted for 14 days; over 4 million shells were fired.

By the time of the first attack on 31 July another factor had come into play. The region is known for its unsettled summer weather, and the summer of 1917 was particularly wet. The ground, torn by shells, soon turned into thick mud, so deep that men and horses drowned in it. The conditions were so bad that Haig suspended the attack on 4 August, but he was still undeterred. The Third Battle of Ypres continued until 18 November, ending with assaults on the ridge and what was left of the village of Passchendaele. The name Passchendaele came to be used for the whole offensive, and for many symbolized the futility of the war on the Western Front. There were over 240,000 British casualties, thousands of whom simply disappeared in the mud.

? EVENT IN QUESTION

What effect did Passchendaele have on the British army?

In his book *The First World War*, the eminent military historian John Keegan wrote: 'On the Somme he [Haig] had sent the flower of British youth to death or mutilation; at Passchendaele he had tipped the survivors into the slough of despond [the depths of despair].' Haig's reasoning for continuing the battle at Ypres is difficult to comprehend; the huge casualties left the British army with no reserves of manpower, and those who did survive had any remaining optimism crushed out of them by their experiences. In a letter, one soldier described '…the mile after mile of the same unending dreariness… whole villages hardly a pile of bricks amongst the mud…' and 'the horror of continual shell fire, rain and mud…'. After the fighting had ended, Haig's chief of staff was taken to visit Passchendaele. It is said that he looked in disbelief and exclaimed: 'My God, did we really send men to fight in this?'

LUDENDORFF'S OFFENSIVE

In March 1918 the Russians signed the Treaty of Brest-Litovsk and the war on the Eastern Front came to an end. This immediately freed German troops and guns to fight on the Western Front. There was some sense of urgency amongst the German high command because in April 1917 the USA had entered the war, and the Germans knew that American troops would soon be joining the Allied forces. The commander of the German army, General Erich von Ludendorff, decided to attack the Allied armies in the spring of 1918 along the Somme. The attacks were designed to push the British army back towards the Channel and the French army towards Paris, creating a gap between the two Allies. Then Ludendorff planned to crush the British forces, in the expectation that France would give up the fight without its ally.

The first attack, code-named Michael, began on 21 March with a bombardment of artillery, smoke and gas shells, machine-gun fire and attacks from the air. By 5 April the Germans had

BELOW *Identifying the bodies of German troops at a makeshift cemetery near the French town of Reims during the Ludendorff Offensive of 1918.*

advanced 32 kilometres along a front of 80 kilometres and created a 16-kilometre gap in the Allied line. However, German casualties were high, and they were advancing across land that they themselves had devastated during the withdrawal to the Hindenburg Line which offered little shelter. Another hazard came in the form of the abandoned supplies of food and drink found by the German invaders, which often proved too tempting. One German officer complained: 'entire divisions totally gorged themselves on food and liquor and failed to press the vital attack forward...'

The apparent success of Operation Michael frightened the Allies and, for the first time, the British and French agreed to unite under the leadership of Field-Marshal Ferdinand Foch, the French Chief of Staff. When the Germans attacked again on 9 April, around Ypres, Haig issued the following order: 'There is no course open to us but to fight it out. Every position must be held to the last man: there must be no retirement. With our backs to the wall and believing in the justice of our cause we must fight on to the end...'

Ludendorff launched more massive attacks in his offensive, along the Aisne and then in July in the Marne region. But American troops were now arriving in their thousands on the front line. Ludendorff's offensive had made massive territorial gains for the Germans, but at a great cost.

? **EVENT IN QUESTION**

Did Ludendorff's offensive strengthen or weaken the German position?

The territory the Germans gained in a few months as a result of Ludendorff's offensive were made at a great human cost – hundreds of thousands of casualties. The only possible replacements for these men were boys just turning 18 and convalescents. But the territorial gains meant that the German front line was longer and more vulnerable than before, therefore needing more men to hold it. Meanwhile thousands of American soldiers were arriving on the Allied front lines. Ludendorff's offensive may have frightened the Allies, and inflicted serious damage on their forces, but it left Germany in a weaker position and it caused the German troops to become increasingly demoralized.

THE ARRIVAL OF THE AMERICANS

When war broke out in 1914 the USA declared itself neutral. So why, three years later, did the Americans go to war on the side of the Allies? The British blockade of the Central Powers (see page 11) forced the Germans to resort to unrestricted submarine warfare – attacking merchant vessels without warning. This led to the sinking of the *Lusitania* in 1915 (see page 11) and the Germans renouncing the policy of attack without warning. But by the beginning of 1917 the situation in Germany was becoming so desperate that the German high command decided to take the risk of starting unrestricted submarine warfare once again. They knew that this move would bring the USA into the war, but they gambled that the Americans would not be able to mobilize fast enough to make a crucial difference.

BELOW *The arrival of American troops in Britain is greeted with great enthusiasm in August 1917. The troops were destined to fight on the Western Front in France.*

In January 1917, the German foreign minister Arthur Zimmermann sent a telegram to the German ambassador in Mexico outlining a plan for Mexico to join the war on Germany's side if the USA entered the war. He also asked for Mexican help to persuade Japan to join the Central Powers against the Allies. He hoped that the USA would end up fighting a war on two fronts against Mexico and Japan, leaving little spare capacity to help the Allies on the Western Front. The Zimmermann telegram was intercepted by the British and its contents sent on to the American government.

ABOVE *American troops in a trench at Ancervilles in France, in March 1918.*

The American president, Woodrow Wilson, declared war on Germany on 6 April 1917 and appointed General John G. Pershing to command the American Expeditionary Force. The first American troops – known as 'doughboys' – began to arrive in France in late 1917, and the first battle involving American forces was at Cantigny in May 1918. Many American divisions fought under British or French command on the Western Front, but in September 1918 the US army went into action as an independent unit at St Mihiel. In the same month American troops joined the French to push the Germans back in the Meuse-Argonne region.

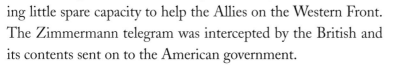

? **EVENT IN QUESTION**

What role the did USA play in bringing war to an end?

According to the historian Allan Millett: 'Although there was little doubt in the minds of the soldiers of the AEF – from General Pershing to the lowliest doughboy – that the Americans had won the war on the Western Front, a more accurate assessment is that the Allies might have lost the war without the American Expeditionary Forces'. When the American soldiers arrived in France many were only half-trained, and all were inexperienced. General Pershing was determined to wait until his troops were trained and ready to form independent units. But he was persuaded to allow American soldiers to serve under British and French commanders as a temporary measure. The influx of fresh troops, however inexperienced, immediately tipped the balance against Germany. It was clear that the American army would become stronger as 1919 approached, helping to convince the Germans that they were defeated on the Western Front.

CHAPTER 3

Fighting the War

THE BRITISH ARMY

When war broke out in 1914 Britain had a small, professional army of about 240,000 regulars, half of whom formed the British Expeditionary Force (BEF) and half of whom were overseas. There was no compulsory military service, but there were reservists and Territorials who could be called on in time of war. The regular soldiers were well-trained and many had had experience of battle in South Africa in the Boer Wars. However, by the end of the First Battle of Ypres (see page 14), most of the original BEF was wiped out.

The drive for new recruits was taken in hand by the Secretary of State for War, Field Marshal Horatio Kitchener, who announced to a startled British government in August 1914 that he expected the war to last for three or four years and that a million men would be needed for the war effort. The government refused to introduce compulsory conscription so Kitchener relied on volunteers. He set about a massive recruitment drive and the result was overwhelming: in all, over three million volunteered to serve in Kitchener's 'new armies'. However, the British army did

BELOW *British volunteers are kitted out with their army uniform. By the end of 1914, a million men had joined Kitchener's 'new armies'.*

not have the manpower to cope with the equipping and training of these civilian volunteers, and many were sent to the Western Front ill-prepared for what awaited them. For many, their first experience of battle was at the Somme in July 1916 (see page 20). The British government finally introduced conscription in February 1916.

ABOVE *German reservists say farewell to their families before leaving Berlin for the front in 1914.*

FRANCE AND GERMANY

Both the French and the Germans had larger regular armies than the British in 1914 because in both countries there was a tradition of military service. France had an army of about 770,000 troops and 46,000 servicemen overseas. Germany's army was made up of about 700,000 men and there were large numbers of reservists who could be called on as soon as the army was mobilized.

US FORCES

The USA joined the war in 1917, and the American government set up a draft system to recruit conscripts to the army. The American Expeditionary Force (AEF) was commanded by General John G. Pershing who, having watched the slaughter on the Western Front from across the Atlantic, was unwilling to turn his troops over to the Allied commanders. In theory, the AEF remained as a separate fighting force in France, although American troops did fight under British and French commanders (see page 29). Unwearied by the long years of the war of attrition that the Allied troops had suffered, the AEF brought much needed reinforcements to the Allied front line. About 2 million American troops served in France; more than 50,000 died in combat.

? EVENT IN QUESTION

Why did so many British men volunteer for service?

The outbreak of war was greeted with a mixture of emotions. Sir Edward Grey made the comment that the war marked 'the lamps going out all over Europe'. Yet there was a great deal of public enthusiasm for the war. When Kitchener launched his recruitment drive, there was a rush to join up – in fact of all the men who volunteered for Kitchener's armies, 29 per cent joined up in the first 8 weeks. The reasons for this rush included a sense of patriotism, a fear of a German invasion of Britain, a sense of adventure, and pressure from friends, wives and sweethearts to 'do your duty for your country'.

TRENCH WARFARE

As the Allies and the Germans fought themselves to a standstill in 1914, soldiers on both sides took refuge in pits and ditches, which they soon enlarged to form continuous trenches. This system of trenches eventually stretched over 540 kilometres, from the North Sea to Switzerland.

NO MAN'S LAND

Between the front line trenches of the opposing sides lay a strip of land that became known as No Man's Land. Both sides positioned rolls of barbed wire in No Man's Land to protect their front lines. The width of No Man's Land varied hugely along the Western Front. On average it was between 100 and 200 metres, but in some places it was as little as 18 metres and in others as wide as 1.6 kilometres. During the day No Man's Land could be eerily silent and still, but at night there was often considerable activity as both sides sent out patrols to spy on the enemy's activities and wiring parties to improve defences. Raiding was also an important part of trench warfare. Groups of raiders would creep through prepared holes in the wire to launch a surprise attack on the opposing front line. The aim was to kill as many of the enemy as possible, to take prisoners and to gain intelligence.

BELOW *Soldiers queue in a trench before launching a raid into No Man's Land. The moment when a soldier left the (relative) safety of the trench to start an attack was known as 'going over the top'.*

TRENCH SYSTEMS

The trench systems of the British, French and Germans varied slightly, but they all made use of a front line, from where attacks were launched, and various supporting trenches dug at intervals parallel to and behind the front line. The British developed a three-tier system of front, support and reserve lines. The front line usually had two trenches, a fire trench and a command trench, connected by communications trenches. The support and reserve lines, behind the front line, were also connected by communications trenches. They accommodated reinforcements for the front line troops. The artillery was situated behind the reserve lines.

The French system was slightly different, with front and support lines, while the Germans built highly sophisticated trench systems. While diagrams of trench systems make them look organized and neat, the reality was often very different. As the war progressed and as trenches were destroyed and re-dug, occupied and abandoned, in some places the front line became maze-like, and fresh troops often needed a guide to direct them to their positions.

BELOW *British soldiers eat part of their daily rations during the Somme offensive.*

? EVENT IN QUESTION

How did soldiers survive life on the Western Front?

One of the ways in which soldiers on both sides of the Western Front made life more bearable was by an unofficial and unspoken policy of 'live and let live'. This was when troops deliberately avoided or restricted aggressive activity in return for the same avoidance or restriction from the enemy. The most basic motive behind this arrangement was a desire to stay alive, rather then to 'kill and be killed'. It also allowed troops to perform the necessities of everyday life; eat hot food, sleep, and delouse themselves (lice were a constant presence in the trenches). 'Live and let live' was strictly forbidden by the high command of both sides, who thought that front line troops should spend their time harassing the enemy. It was, nevertheless, a fact of life on many parts of the front throughout the war.

WEAPONS OF WAR

The main weapon for the infantry (foot-soldiers) was the rifle. Every soldier had a rifle equipped with a bayonet, a sharp blade that was attached to the end of the rifle for use in attacks. Troops in the front line had to be constantly on guard against snipers in the enemy lines. If an unwary soldier allowed his head to show above the top of the trench, he was likely to be killed by a bullet through the skull. Troops used periscopes to peer over the edge of the trench to view No Man's Land and the enemy front line beyond, but even the lens of a periscope was a target for a sharpshooter. Snipers' rifles could also be fixed on a position where it was known that lookout was kept, so that sniping could continue at night.

BELOW *German troops rifle training during the early days of the war.*

Troops were also issued with grenades and bombs for use in attack, but the other main front-line weapon was the machine-gun. This weapon could fire continuous rounds of bullets loaded on to a belt – from 250 to 600 rounds a minute depending upon the type of gun. The gun was mounted on a fixed tripod and was manned by a crew of between six and ten men. It could be set to fire on a fixed trajectory along the enemy's front line, so in the

ABOVE *German machine-gun crew in a trench on the Western Front.*

event of an attack the crew simply had to man the gun as fast as possible and start firing. The drawback of the machine-gun was that it was heavy and not easily movable, and it needed a large crew to fire it – although there are tales of one solitary machine-gunner heroically operating his weapon until the last.

Behind the trenches lay the big guns – the artillery – manned by teams of gunners. It was the artillery and their shells that caused most casualties along the Western Front. The artillery were used to prepare for battle by firing planned bombardments, such as the one before the Third Battle of Ypres (see page 25). The big guns could also respond to new information from the front line, pinpointing an exact location for shelling the enemy. They also needed to react quickly to an SOS call – usually signal lights – if the front line was under attack.

(see page 25)

? EVENT IN QUESTION

What were the pros and cons of a preliminary bombardment?

The Allied policy of using artillery gave notice to the enemy that an attack was going to happen in a particular place along the front line. And while day after day of heavy shelling undoubtedly had an effect on the morale of the Germans, because of the strength of the German defences it usually did not force them to abandon their positions as the Allies intended. The impact of thousands of shells exploding on the ground created huge holes – not ideal for the attackers, who had to navigate their way through and around the craters. It also made it difficult for the artillery to be moved forward to provide cover for an advancing army. Nevertheless, the Allied high command remained unwilling to launch an attack without the precaution of a preliminary bombardment.

German nurses wear gas masks as they treat two victims of an Allied gas attack.

NEW TACTICS

Almost as soon as the trenches were dug, inventors began to devise new weapons and technologies for use on the Western Front. It soon became clear that fresh ideas were going to be needed to try to break the deadlock between the two sides. The British government was bombarded with ideas for new and improved weapons, only a very few of which were accepted for use in the trenches. One of these was the trench mortar, designed by F.W. Stokes. This weapon allowed bombs to be fired from the trenches and by 1916 there were three different types, the largest of which could send a 70-kilogram bomb up to a kilometre. While trench mortars allowed a more rapid and accurate response to any enemy activity than an SOS call to the artillery, the infantry were wary of these weapons. They were so effective that they tended to provoke angry retaliation from the enemy, as one military historian recorded: 'owing to the retaliation provoked by their use, those operating them [trench mortars] were very unpopular with the occupants of the various trenches…'

Other new technologies that came into use were aircraft (see page 40), tanks (see page 42) and gas. The first use of gas on the Western Front was by the Germans on 22 April 1915 at Langemarck, north of Ypres, during the Second Battle of Ypres. The Germans released 5,000 cylinders of chlorine gas that drifted on the wind over the Allied trenches. Thousands of French troops fled as the gas choked them, and many died. Crude gas masks were quickly improvized to try to protect front line troops from similar attacks. However the Allies were also developing their own poison gases, and they first used gas in an attack at Loos on 15 September 1915.

One notable tactical innovation introduced during the war on the Western Front was the 'creeping barrage'. This tactic used the artillery to protect the infantry and to 'neutralise' the enemy during an attack. It was introduced during 1916, and the principle was that a wall of shells should fall just ahead of the attacking troops. This wall moved forwards by a few yards every few minutes, followed as fast as possible by the attacking soldiers. The aim was to keep the enemy pinned down in their trenches, unable to man their rifles and machine guns. It relied heavily on the accuracy of the artillery – who of course could not see what they were firing at (see page 38). Nevertheless it became an important tactic in offensives along the Western Front.

? EVENT IN QUESTION

How effective was gas?

Both the Allies used various forms of gas: chlorine, the more lethal phosgene, and mustard gas, which burned and blistered the skin and often caused temporary blindness. Mustard gas was first used by the Germans in July 1917, to great effect. However, by 1916, both sides had introduced gas masks as standard issue, which gave the infantry some protection against these attacks. Gas attacks were difficult to manage, because once the canisters were opened a change in the wind could easily blow the gas back on to the attacker's own front line. Throughout the war, gas tended to incapacitate more troops than it killed – nevertheless it was a useful tactic because it removed large numbers of troops from the front line while they recovered.

ABOVE *A German soldier uses a field telephone to send information during the fighting at Verdun.*

COMMUNICATIONS

In the age of radio, television, the internet and the mobile phone, it is difficult to grasp how basic the means of communication were during the First World War. Relaying commands and information from one part of the battlefield to another, or from headquarters and back, was one of the biggest challenges faced by both sides on the Western Front. Wireless radio sets were being developed during the war, but they were very large and heavy – needing 12 men to transport all the necessary apparatus.

The main form of communication from the front line back to headquarters and to other areas of the front line was by telephone. Wires were laid beneath the ground in places where they were less likely to be broken by shelling – experience showed that they needed to be at least 1.8 metres below the surface to be completely safe. However, burying cable so deep was time-consuming work, and once the cable was in place it could not easily be moved. The system worked reasonably well, though, until an attack was launched. As attacking soldiers moved forwards towards the enemy, they were inevitably moving further away from the nearest point of communication. Troops unwound telephone cable as they attacked, but it was nearly always broken during the fighting. Other methods of communication included signalling lamps, human runners, pigeon post, and even message-carrying dogs.

One vital area of communications was between the front line and the artillery. The gunners who manned the artillery usually fired without being able to see their targets – if they could see the enemy they could also be seen and were vulnerable. They relied on information from observation posts along the front line, and later in the war from observation balloons and aircraft. The problem was that once the telephone lines were broken, messages only travelled as fast as a human runner, or if visibility was good

enough a flag signaller could be used. In order to set their guns the artillery used maps of the front and aerial photographs, taken from aircraft. Aircraft and observers in balloons were also used to check that the shells were falling in the correct area during an attack.

ABOVE *This messenger dog was used to carry food to German troops on the front line.*

? EVENT IN QUESTION

How big a part did the difficulties of communications on the front line play in the war of attrition?

Difficulties in communications meant that it was much easier for defenders, falling back to their reserve trenches, to make a coherent plan, than for attackers to communicate with each other and with their commanders. As it was most often the Allies who were on the offensive, this became a particular problem for them. Commanders such as Sir Douglas Haig have often been accused of being out of touch with the reality of what was happening on the Western Front, and of failing to react quickly enough to events during battle. But it could take many hours for a message to travel from the front line back to headquarters – by which time the situation on the front could have changed completely. It was difficult, therefore, for plans to be adapted according to circumstance, and probably partly explains why most attacks on the Western Front ended indecisively or in failure.

WAR IN THE AIR

Troops sheltering in the trenches of the Western Front were sometimes entertained by dog-fights between German and Allied aircraft in the air above the front line. Often these fights ended in the crash of one or both planes and the inevitable death of the pilots. Pilots were not equipped with parachutes, and in 1917 the life expectancy of a new British pilot was between 11 days and three weeks. In 1914 the British Royal Flying Corps had just 63 machines – by 1918 the newly formed Royal Air Force had 22,000 aircraft.

The primary function of aeroplanes during the First World War was reconaissance and observation – artillery-spotting, shooting down enemy observation balloons and similar tasks. Their work was vital to produce the maps and aerial images of the Western Front needed by the artillery, and to plan attacks. As the Germans had the advantage of the high ground along much of the Western Front, dominating the air became an important strategy for the Allies. However, the Germans responded by sending up their own planes to stop the Allied aerial activities. This led to the development of fighting techniques in the air.

At first pilots took small guns with them to shoot at their enemies. Then in 1915, a French pilot, Roland Garros, devised a way of fixing a machine-gun on to his plane. But after a few weeks he crashed behind the German front line, and his invention was adapted by the Dutch engineer Anthony Fokker for the Germans. By 1916 both sides were using similar technology and aerial combat led to the development of fast 'fighter' planes such as the Sopwith Camel.

Pilots who survived for any length of time were acclaimed as heroes. These air 'aces' included the German Manfred von Richthofen, the French pilot Georges Guynemer, and the British pilots Albert Ball and Edward 'Mick' Mannock, all of whom were shot down and killed. American pilots also flew on the Western Front before the USA entered the war, as part of the 'Escadrille Americaine' founded in 1916 and made up of American volunteers who were keen to see action in France.

By 1917, both sides started to use aircraft to attack troops on the ground and developed bombers for attacks on the Western Front and on the home fronts. The Germans used lighter-than-air dirigibles (air balloons) called Zeppelins to mount bombing raids on London from 1915 onwards. They later used Gotha bombers for air raids, while the British developed the Handley-Page bomber.

ABOVE *Aerial combat in the skies above the Western Front: a British plane shoots down its German enemy in 1918.*

❓ PEOPLE IN QUESTION

Manfred von Richthofen (1882–1918)

The German flying 'ace' Manfred von Richthofen started the war in a cavalry regiment. In 1915, bored with the inactivity of the trenches, he joined the German air service. He became very interested in the management and organization of aerial combat. He acquired the nickname the 'Red Baron' because of the colour of his Fokker plane, and was credited with shooting down 80 enemy planes before his own death on 21 April 1918. There are two accounts of his death; that he was shot down by anti-aircraft fire from the ground, or that he was shot down by Captain A. Roy Brown, a Canadian serving in the Royal Air Force.

A Belgian armoured car which would have been used at the beginning of the war. Later in the war tanks replaced armoured cars.

THE ALLIED SECRET WEAPON

As early as autumn 1914 the British government began to look into the possibility of inventing some kind of vehicle that could cross trenches, break through barbed wire and eliminate machine-guns. During 1915 both the British and the French developed the first tanks, although they worked independently on these projects. The word 'tank' came from the crates that the British used to transport these secret machines to France – they were originally called 'land-ships' but this name soon died out. The French called their tanks 'chars' (chariots).

The leading role in the development of tanks in Britain was taken by Colonel Ernest Swinton. He was very enthusiastic about this new invention, and had definite ideas about how it should be used. He said that tanks should not appear on the battlefield until there were enough of them to make an impact, and to take the enemy completely by surprise. He also thought that they should support the infantry in an attack, breaking a hole in the enemy line to allow the soldiers to pour through. He was ignored, however. General Douglas Haig was keen to make use of even the few tanks that were ready by the summer of 1916, and so the Allies' secret weapon made its debut at the Somme on 15 September 1916.

It wasn't a complete success. Although the appearance of 36 tanks terrified the unsuspecting German troops, nearly all the tanks broke down or became stuck in rough ground. Nevertheless, Haig was impressed enough with their performance to order 1,000 more tanks to be built. However, it was not until November 1917 that tanks made the impact on the battlefield that Colonel Swinton had in mind. At the Battle of Cambrai the Allies used over 350 tanks in a massed attack against the German front line. This was the first time that tanks formed a key part of the plan of attack and it was initially very successful. After a short, intense artillery bombardment the tanks led the attack, followed closely by the infantry. Most of the German troops simply fled, and by the end of the day church bells rang out in Britain to signal an Allied victory. However, the Germans counter-attacked, and by the end of the battle in early December little ground was gained on either side.

? EVENT IN QUESTION

Were tanks a war-winning weapon?

The Germans built a few prototype tanks but then decided that tanks were too unreliable and concentrated their efforts on other technology. Indeed, British tanks were slow and too liable to break down to be truly effective. More reliable were the French Renault tanks, which were lighter and faster. Nevertheless, after the lessons learned at the Battle of Cambrai, tanks went on to play an important role in the battles of 1918. Tanks were most useful when used in close coordination with the artillery and infantry. They were not, however, a war-winning weapon in their own right, nor did they offer a solution to the stalemate on the Western Front.

BELOW *A tank in use on the Western Front. Tanks played an important part in the later battles of the war.*

RIGHT *Anti-German
propaganda on the cover
of a French magazine
of 1915.*

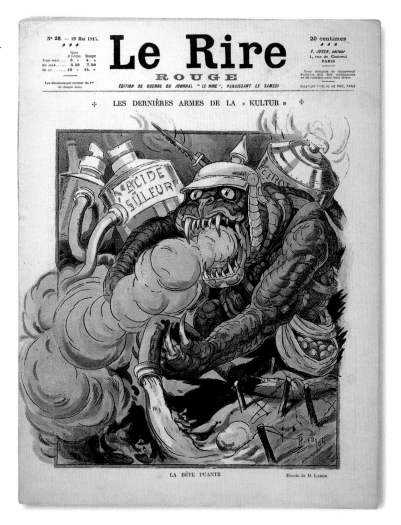

REPORTING THE WAR

So much is known about the First World War today, and information is so readily available, that it is difficult to believe how little information about the Western Front battles reached people at home during the war itself. As soon as war broke out, governments moved to censor the press. In Britain the Defence of the Realm Act was passed on 8 August 1914. It forbade the publishing of any information that could be of use to the enemy as well as news that could undermine loyalty to the king, or affect recruitment. Similar laws were also passed in France and Germany. The problem for newspapers was that information of use to the enemy covered almost anything – from troop movements to weather reports.

At the beginning of the war Lord Kitchener, Minister for War in Britain (see page 30), banned war correspondents from a set zone around the BEF in France. Instead a Press Bureau was set up that received reports from the military, censored them and then issued them to the press. As battles raged across Belgium and northern France the gap between the reality of the war and the news bulletins began to widen. Some war correspondents decided to risk arrest, or worse, and set off across northern France to try to establish what was really happening.

The strict censorship of news caused a major problem for the government, however. On one hand people at home were being urged to help the war effort by signing up for service, manufacturing munitions and other war work – on the other hand very little of the seriousness of the situation in France actually reached the newspapers. The government needed the support of the general public, and the press was very influential in forming the opinion of the public. Accordingly, in May 1915 five accredited war correspondents were allowed to travel to and report on the Western Front. They wore uniform and were accompanied at all times by an official censor. Their reports continued to downplay the negative aspects of war, and to recount stories of heroism and valour. The general public relied on rumours, on letters from their loved ones at the front (also censored), and on the accounts of those home on leave for news of the truth of the war.

? EVENT IN QUESTION

Why did the general public accept such huge casualty figures?

'If the people really knew, the war would be stopped tomorrow. But of course they don't – and can't know. The correspondents don't write and the censorship would not pass the truth.' These words of the British Prime Minister David Lloyd George give a clue about the public acceptance of casualty figures. The public didn't know the truth, and the reality of battles such as the Somme or Passchendaele didn't become fully known until the 1920s. Dispatches sent on 1 July 1916 were vague but optimistic: 'It is too early to as yet to give anything but the barest particulars, as the fighting is developing in intensity, but the British troops have already occupied the German front line. Many prisoners have already fallen into our hands, and as far as can be ascertained our casualties have not been heavy.' In fact, 20,000 British troops died on that day alone (see page 21).

Life on the Western Front

CHRISTMAS 1914

The winter of 1914 was wet, cold and utterly miserable for the troops sheltering in the muddy trenches of the Western Front. But Christmas Day 1914 dawned cold and frosty, freezing the mud solid and coating everything with a dazzling white frost. The previous night there had been singing in the trenches, 'Stille Nacht', 'O Come All Ye Faithful', and 'Minuit, Chrétiens' drifting across the cold air. As day dawned, and the sun gradually burned away the early morning mist, the soldiers got out of the trenches and began to walk about, warming themselves up.

BELOW *German troops celebrate Christmas in the trenches.*

It soon became clear that the enemy soldiers were doing likewise, and it didn't take long before British and German, and French and German, were meeting in No Man's Land. The enemy soldiers exchanged Christmas greetings, and gave each other small gifts of cigarettes, cigars, chocolates and buttons. Some soldiers even went into the enemy trenches; others took group photos to commemorate the occasion. In some places impromptu games of football were played. In others, troops took advantage of the truce to bury the corpses of dead comrades that lay in No Man's Land. Throughout the day not a shot was fired.

One British soldier described the Christmas Day truce in a letter home to his family: 'On that day [Christmas Day] everyone spontaneously left their trenches and had a meeting halfway between the trenches. Germans gave us cigars, and we gave them chocolate and tobacco. They seemed very pleased to see us!' In fact, the Christmas truces were part of the more prevalent 'live and let live' system that was an element of everyday life in the trenches (see page 33). In many places the Christmas truce went on for days, without any shots being fired from either side. As usual this peace met with official disapproval, however, and orders came for the truce to stop. A British soldier wrote on 30 December: 'Same routine as before. Still no war! At about lunchtime however a message came down the line to say that [the] Germans had sent across to say that their General was coming along in the afternoon, so we had better keep down, as they might have to do a little shooting to make things look right!!! This we did, and a few shots came over about 3.30 p.m.'

? EVENT IN QUESTION

Why did the Allied and German commanders ban any future fraternization?

When word of the unofficial Christmas truce reached the commanders of the Allied and German armies, they were not amused. Orders were issued to prevent such a truce happening again, as well as orders for raids and attacks along the line. High command wanted their soldiers to show 'offensive spirit' and aggression to the enemy. They knew that fraternization between soldiers on the two sides only served to underline the similarities between them – especially the similarities of hardships endured in the trenches. In order to try to keep the level of aggression up, specialist units were sometimes sent into the front line with the intention of stirring up some action by attacking and irritating the enemy. But, despite all the efforts of the high command on both sides, the 'live and let live' policy, of which the Christmas truces were just one example, continued along the Western Front throughout the war.

ABOVE *French soldiers relax in an underground shelter in the trenches.*

IN THE TRENCHES

The experience of daily life in the trenches depended largely on whether a soldier found himself on an 'active' or 'quiet' section of the front line. In active areas, the two sides were constantly antagonizing each other with snipers' bullets, raids, mortar shells and bombs. Life in these sectors of the front line was difficult, dangerous and wearing on the nerves, and casualties could be high. In 'quiet' sectors life was safer, if often monotonous, revolving around some kind of daily routine.

A typical day would start at dawn with 'Stand To', when guard would be kept in case of any attack or aggression from the enemy. The order 'Stand Down' signalled time for breakfast. Food was vitally important for the men on the front line, and rations were usually plentiful. Water came from water carts, or from local farms or pumps. Many soldiers slept during the day, as night-time was the most important time for activity. But others did jobs during the day such as repairing trenches, laying down duckboards or digging dugouts. Lunch was the main meal of the day, after which there could be more duties, called 'fatigues', or guard duty, or sleep. Tea was followed by 'Stand To' as dusk fell, and then as the order to 'Stand Down' came, work started for the night. Night-time was when patrols went out into No Man's Land to lay wire, or to cut wire in preparation for an attack, and to collect the wounded or dead bodies for burial if possible. It was also a time to try to spy on the enemy, as well as completing work on the trenches that could not safely be done by day.

Even in 'quiet' sectors, life in the trenches was hardly comfortable. Many men put on a brave face in their letters home, a few positively enjoyed the danger, but for many the experience was intolerable and pointless. One artillery officer wrote to his wife in 1916: 'Charming life this is. Both sides bury themselves in mudholes and peep at each other through slits in the earth. Occasionally one side or the other has a bombardment which consists of blowing off £10,000 worth of ammunition and killing no men. Then they retire to their holes to lick their sores like two dogs after a fight.'

RIGHT *The trenches were almost constantly wet and muddy, despite pumping and baling devices.*

? EVENT IN QUESTION

Why did men put up with the conditions on the front?

The trenches were unhealthy places. The constant mud and water – sometimes waist deep – gave many soldiers 'trench foot' – when the feet literally rotted inside the boots. In 'active' sectors, the sound of gunfire and explosions of shells, lack of sleep and constant danger left many men with broken nerves, a condition that became known as 'shell-shock'. In the filthy conditions of the trenches, diseases such as dysentery and 'trench fever' were also widespread. So why did men put up with such conditions? Partly, the strict military discipline of the army gave them little or no choice, partly shared experiences created an intense comradeship between the men in the front line which helped them to carry on in the face of adversity. There were also day-to-day matters such as warm clothes, adequate food, the ration of alcohol, and leave from the trenches, all of which were relatively mundane but nevertheless extremely important for the well-being of the front-line soldier.

COMMANDERS AND COMMANDED

While the ordinary soldiers of the British, French and German armies coped with the day-to-day realities of life in the trenches, their commanders lived in safety and some luxury, well behind the front lines. The British Commander-in-Chief, General Haig, was based for much of the war at a chateau near Montreuil in northern France. Here he lived in splendour, certainly compared to the conditions endured by the men under his command. Most afternoons he went for a ride on his immaculately groomed horse, on roads specially sanded to prevent the horse's hooves from slipping. The war correspondent Philip Gibbs frequently witnessed Haig setting off for his daily ride, and could not help contrasting what he saw with the horrors of the front line, roughly 90 kilometres away: 'One often saw the Commander-in-Chief [Haig] starting for an afternoon ride, a fine figure, nobly mounted, with

BELOW *Members of the German high command relax in comfort after a good dinner.*

two ADCs [aides-de-camp] and an escort of Lancers. A pretty sight, with fluttering pennons [flags] on their lances and horses groomed to the last hair. It was prettier than the real thing up in the Salient [Ypres] or beyond the Somme, where dead bodies lay on upheaved earth among ruins and slaughtered trees. War at Montreuil was quite a pleasant experience for elderly generals...'

The British Prime Minister David Lloyd George wrote that 'the solicitude with which most generals in high places (there were honourable exceptions) avoided personal jeopardy is one of the debatable novelties of modern warfare...' It is certainly true that much of the high command had little idea about the true conditions in the trenches, and made plans of attack with little conception of the realities for the men on the ground. However, some generals did expose themselves to danger, and were prepared to stand up for their men if they thought a plan was ill-conceived. It could also be argued that it was necessary for commanders to stay away from the front line in order to be best placed to receive communications and to try to piece together a broader picture of what was going on, away from the heat of battle.

? EVENT IN QUESTION

Why was high command so out of touch with the realities of life on the front line?

The stark contrasts in living conditions and in the dangers endured between those in command and those being commanded did not go unnoticed by the men at the front. As the war developed, many ordinary front line soldiers began to feel more sympathy and affinity with their enemy counterparts than with their own, distant commanders. One British soldier voiced his feelings in the following words: 'When one is in the front line one cannot help having a fairly deep sympathy for the wretched fellow in the other front line across 'no-man's-land'; one knows that he is going through just as many dangers and discomforts, and that he is simply carrying out the orders of some general whose dangers and discomforts are infinitely less, and the hatred you both have towards these generals breeds a common sympathy that is irresistible...'

ABOVE *A firing squad prepares to carry out the execution of spies who were found guilty of assisting the Germans during the war. This execution occurred after the war, in 1920, but similar firing squads were used for executions during the war.*

DESERTION

For some soldiers, life in the front line became so intolerable that they simply ran away. This was known as desertion, and in the British army it was punishable by death. Another means of leaving the front line was a self-inflicted wound, for example in the foot. However, this was risky because if the wound could be proved to be self-inflicted it also became a crime punishable by death. During the First World War, the British army sentenced 3,080 of its own soldiers to death for charges including desertion, cowardice, sleeping while on duty and disobedience. Of these, 346 executions were carried out by firing squad, the remainder were mostly sentenced to hard labour. It is likely that at least some who were judged to be 'cowards' were simply suffering from acute shell-shock and were unable to continue. The Australians refused to allow any of their troops to be executed, despite protestations from General Haig. There were far fewer death sentences in either the French or German armies, although the French army suffered the most serious mutinies of the war.

MUTINY

The French mutinies happened during the Nivelle Offensive (see page 23), as soon as it became clear that, despite Nivelle's promises, the attack was a failure. Although supposed to last for no longer than 48 hours, and despite huge casualties, Nivelle insisted that the offensive continue. While no front-line troops mutinied, when ordered back to the front, many French soldiers simply refused to go. The mutinies continued throughout May 1917 and into early June. Nivelle was sacked in mid-May and replaced by General Pétain who set about restoring order.

> ### ? EVENT IN QUESTION
>
> ### *What provoked the French army to mutiny in 1917?*
>
> The French mutinies were serious, coming as they did at such a critical point of the war. Many politicians were deeply suspicious of the protesting soldiers, suspecting a revolutionary plot. But it seems that the mutinying troops had simply had enough of being ordered to do the impossible – and going on strike was the only way they could express their grievances. There was certainly no intention to allow the Germans to win the war as a result of the mutinies.
>
> Pétain listened to the soldiers' grievances as well as imposing military discipline. 3,427 French soldiers were court-martialled, and 554 sentenced to death. Of these, 49 were actually shot. General Haig considered this too lenient and remarked that 'Pétain ought to have shot 2,000'. At the same time, Pétain visited his troops and made various promises. Conditions in the trenches would be improved, and a system of leave and rest set up. There would be no more major attacks on the scale of the Nivelle Offensive; instead the French would wait for 'the Americans and the tanks'. In accordance with these promises, Pétain instituted a more defensive policy along the French front line. Amazingly, the Germans failed to realize what was going on in the French army, and to capitalize on its disarray.

CHAPTER 5

The End of the War

The attack on the Marne (the Second Battle of the Marne) that formed the last part of Ludendorff's Offensive (see page 27) came to an end on 17 July 1918. Ludendorff now knew that he had lost too many men to be able to make up his losses, and he called off plans for another offensive in Flanders. This was the beginning of the end for the Germans.

THE ALLIED ADVANCE

BELOW *A group of American soldiers pose with a German machine gun captured during the St Mihiel offensive in 1918.*

The Allies had suffered greatly during Ludendorff's Offensive, but they had also learned valuable lessons. Now united under the French Chief of Staff, Field-Marshal Ferdinand Foch, they began to plan a series of attacks to drive the Germans back. These attacks were successful partly because of new tactics such as surprising the enemy, large-scale use of tanks (as seen at Cambrai),

and better liaison between tanks, infantry and artillery. Communications were also slightly improved thanks to the use of radio sets (see page 38). But the overwhelming factor in the Allies' favour was the Americans. The numbers of American troops arriving on the Western Front by 1918 was deeply disturbing for the Germans, and sapped the already low morale of the German soldiers.

The Allies launched the first of their counter-offensives on 8 August. It was spearheaded by Canadian and Australian troops near Amiens and was an immediate success. Ludendorff wrote in his diary that 'August the 8th was a black day for the German Army in the history of this war.' Thousands of Germans surrendered with little resistance. The counter-offensive rolled on and by 9 September the Allies had recovered all the ground lost during Ludendorff's Offensive. Disillusionment about the war had spread to Germany too, where people on the home front were starving as a result of the Allied blockade of Germany. When new conscripts arrived on the front line they were accused of being strike-breakers, and prolonging the war.

Nevertheless, the Germans did not give up easily and the fighting continued throughout September at St Mihiel and in the Meuse-Argonne region where there were heavy Allied casualties. On 29 September Ludendorff finally admitted to the Kaiser (German king) that he thought the war was lost. The German government wrote to President Wilson requesting an armistice, but when the reply came the terms were considered too harsh. Ludendorff began to reconsider his position and demanded that the war should continue. It was, however, too late.

? EVENT IN QUESTION

General Erich von Ludendorff (1865 – 1937)

Together with General Paul von Hindenburg, Ludendorff had virtually controlled Germany since 1916. After that date, these two men took all the major German decisions of the war, including the resumption of unrestricted submarine warfare and the launch of the Ludendorff Offensive. Ludendorff gambled everything when he ordered these attacks on the Western Front in 1918. On 28 September 1918 when it became clear that they – and he – had failed, Ludendorff descended into a hysterical rage and collapsed, although reports of these events were later denied. But Germany still had a relatively determined army in strong defensive positions occupying more land than before the war, and the Allies were not yet advancing. Although outright victory was unlikely, a skilled diplomat may have been able to negotiate favourable peace terms for Germany. But Ludendorff was no diplomat, he had fought for victory for Germany; and now that was out of his grasp he started to look for ways to divert the blame away from himself.

CONFLICT IN GERMANY

When Ludendorff met with the Kaiser on 29 September 1918 he requested that a new democratic government should be formed in Germany. It would be up to the members of this new government to negotiate an armistice with the Allies, and the shame of Germany's defeat would fall squarely on the civilian government and not on the army. Despite having been in effective control of Germany for the previous two years, Ludendorff made the following extraordinary statement: 'I have asked His Majesty to bring those people into the government who are largely responsible that things have turned out as they have. We shall therefore see these gentlemen enter the ministries, and they must now make the peace which has to be made. They must now eat the soup they have ladled out to us.'

TOWARDS ARMISTICE

BELOW *Allied troops on the bank of the St Quentin Canal in September 1918.*

The new German government based its request for peace on a document drawn up in January 1918 by the American president, Woodrow Wilson. It was known as the 'Fourteen Points' because it listed fourteen terms on which an honourable peace and new world order could be based. But when the Allies replied to the German request, the German government considered the terms

too harsh. Ludendorff, who had by now recovered his nerve, began to demand that the Germans should continue to fight for victory. The tensions between a government trying to negotiate peace terms and a general trying to continue the war became too much and on 26 October Ludendorff was forced to resign.

Meanwhile the fighting continued across northern France. At the end of September, Allied troops approached the Hindenburg Line and took the St Quentin Canal. Throughout October the Allies continued to push the Germans back, although casualties remained high.

The Allied leaders met in Paris to discuss an armistice. While the British and French were mostly in favour of bringing an end to the fighting, the American commander General John Pershing thought that the Allies should force the Germans into an unconditional surrender. This was not to happen, however. On 8 November, in a special train in the Forest of Compiegne near Paris, the Allied leader General Foch met with a German delegation. After days of negotiation, the armistice was signed at 5 a.m. on 11 November 1918. Fighting stopped on the Western Front at 11 a.m. on the same day.

? EVENT IN QUESTION

Was the German army 'stabbed in the back'?

The German army marched home from the Western Front looking to all intents and purposes like an undefeated force. Indeed, many people in Germany believed that the army had not been defeated in the field, but that it had been betrayed by the German government. Of course, shifting the blame for defeat was Ludendorff's intention, and the rumour that the army had been 'stabbed in the back' by the civilian government suited his purposes perfectly. In fact, if the army had been stabbed in the back by anyone, it was by its own commander. Nevertheless, the legend that the army had been betrayed by civilian socialists, Jews and pacifists continued to circulate, and this lie eventually came to contribute to the rise to power of Adolf Hitler, and the start of the next catastrophic war.

RIGHT *The end of the war is greeted with joy and relief by the French people. A wounded Canadian soldier stands among the crowd.*

WAR GUILT

The armistice signed on 11 November imposed many conditions on the defeated Germans. Within two weeks the Germans had to evacuate all captured territory, as well as Alsace and Lorraine, which became French territories once more. They also had to hand over vast amounts of equipment – enough to ensure that the fighting could not continue – to release all prisoners of war, and to pay war reparations.

Of the nations involved in the fighting on the Western Front, only the USA profited economically from the war. Britain, France and Germany all had huge war debts, and in addition France had suffered terrible devastation in the areas where battles had raged. All the participants on the Western Front had suffered thousands upon thousands of casualties, and the sense of loss and grief would take a long time to heal. It is not surprising, then, that many people in the victorious countries thought that Germany should be made to pay for the war.

? EVENT IN QUESTION

Who won the war?

The simple answer to this question is the Allies, who were able to dictate terms and conditions to the defeated Germans. But as time went on, many people in Germany came to believe that the war had ended in a draw between the two sides, with the balance of power shared equally. No part of the German homeland had been occupied during the war, and Germany was left with its industry intact, although its economy, like those of Britain and France, was in ruins. France had reclaimed its lost territories of Alsace and Lorraine, but its priority still remained security against invasion from its still-powerful neighbour. Britain had gained little or nothing from the war, while the USA emerged from the war with a new position as the biggest creditor nation in the world.

Negotiations for peace opened in January 1919, in Paris. Although 32 nations were represented, the decisions were effectively taken by just four men (the 'Council of Four'), the British Prime Minister David Lloyd George, the French president Georges Clemenceau, the American president Woodrow Wilson and the Italian premier Vittorio Orlando. The Germans were not included in the negotiations. The Treaty of Versailles was signed on 28 June 1919 in the Hall of Mirrors at the Palace of Versailles. The most controversial part of the Treaty was Article 231, known as the 'War Guilt Clause'. It forced Germany to accept responsibility for starting the war, and therefore for paying huge war reparations to the Allies. The final figure for these reparations was not decided until 1921. Germany also lost territory both in Europe and all its overseas colonies, its army was reduced in size, conscription forbidden, and its fleet surrendered to Britain.

The German public was outraged by the Treaty of Versailles, and those who had signed it on their behalf became known by many as 'the criminals of 1919'. Whether or not the Treaty of Versailles was a just settlement, it was viewed in Germany as unreasonably harsh, and it helped the growth of the nationalist movement in Germany. In Britain, a growing belief that the Treaty was too harsh also helped to foster the policy of appeasement towards Germany in the 1930s. The course was set for another war.

BELOW *Makeshift wooden crosses mark the graves of dead American soldiers in 1918.*

1914

28 JUNE Assassination of Archduke Franz Ferdinand and his wife in Sarajevo.

23 JULY Austria-Hungary issues ultimatum to Serbia.

28 JULY Austria-Hungary declares war on Serbia.

30 JULY Russia mobilizes its army.

1 AUGUST Germany declares war on Russia.

3 AUGUST Germany declares war on France.

4 AUGUST German troops invade Belgium.

4 AUGUST Britain declares war on Germany.

9 AUGUST First British troops land in France.

20 AUGUST Germans capture Brussels.

23-24 AUGUST Battle of Mons.

26 AUGUST Moltke diverts troops to East Prussia.

2 SEPTEMBER French government leaves Paris.

4-10 SEPTEMBER Battle of the Marne.

9 SEPTEMBER Moltke orders Germans to retreat to River Aisne.

12-18 SEPTEMBER First Battle of the Aisne.

MID SEPTEMBER-LATE OCTOBER 'Race for the Sea'.

14 SEPTEMBER General Erich von Falkenhayn takes over from Moltke.

MID OCTOBER-MID NOVEMBER First Battle of Ypres.

NOVEMBER Construction of trench system begins.

1915

10-13 MARCH Allied attack at Neuve Chapelle.

22 APRIL Start of Second Battle of Ypres: Germans use gas on front line for first time.

7 MAY Sinking of *Lusitania* by German U-boat.

15 SEPTEMBER First use of gas by Allies at Loos.

18 DECEMBER General Douglas Haig replaces Sir John French.

20 DECEMBER Falkenhayn proposes Verdun attack.

1916

21 FEBRUARY Operation Gericht marks beginning of fighting at Verdun.

24 JUNE Preliminary bombardment of German lines begins on the Somme.

1 JULY-19 NOVEMBER Battle of the Somme.

29 AUGUST Ludendorff and Hindenburg replace Falkenhayn.

15 SEPTEMBER First use of tanks on the battlefield.

1917

16 MARCH Start of Operation Alberich as Germans withdraw to Hindenburg Line.

6 APRIL USA declares war on Germany.

9 APRIL Battle of Arras starts with capture of Vimy Ridge.

16 APRIL Nivelle Offensive in the Champagne region.

MAY-JUNE French mutinies.

15 MAY General Henri Pétain takes over from Nivelle.

7 JUNE Mines detonated on Messines Ridge.

17 JULY Preliminary bombardment begins at Ypres.

31 JULY-18 NOVEMBER Third Battle of Ypres (Passchendaele).

20 NOVEMBER First successful use of tanks at Battle of Cambrai.

1918
JANUARY Wilson draws up 'Fourteen Points'.

3 MARCH Treaty of Brest-Litovsk marks end of war on Eastern Front.

21 MARCH Operation Michael marks start of Ludendorff's Offensive.

APRIL Ludendorff's second offensive in Flanders.

MAY-JUNE Ludendorff's third offensive in the Aisne.

28 MAY US troops see action for first time at Cantigny.

JULY Second Battle of the Marne.

8 AUGUST Allied counter-offensives begin.

SEPTEMBER-NOVEMBER Allied offensives in Meuse-Argonne region.

SEPTEMBER AEF fights as an independent force at St Mihiel.

29 SEPTEMBER Allied forces cross St Quentin Canal.

9 OCTOBER Allied forces cross Hindenburg Line.

26 OCTOBER Ludendorff forced to resign.

8 NOVEMBER Allies meet German armistice delegation in Forest of Compiegne.

11 NOVEMBER Armistice starts at 11 a.m.

61

Glossary

appeasement foreign policy based on diplomacy and negotiation with hostile states in an attempt to avoid war.

armaments weapons.

armistice an agreement between enemy sides to suspend hostilities.

arms race the 'race' beween two opposing nations to accumulate more and more powerful weapons.

Balkans the Balkan States in the south-east part of Europe.

blockade the use of military force by one nation to prevent access to an enemy nation's ports or other key supply points.

cavalry a regiment of mounted troops.

censor someone who controls the exchange of information, for example in the newspapers, in personal letters, etc.

Central Powers a term denoting the alliance of Germany and Austria-Hungary during the First World War.

conscription compulsory military service. Those called up as a result of conscription are known as conscripts.

convalescent someone who is recovering from an illness or injury.

court martial a military court where people are tried according to military law.

creeping barrage one of the tactical innovations introduced on the Western Front. The principle was that a wall of shells should fall just ahead of attacking troops in order to neutralize the enemy.

delegation a group of people chosen to represent others.

democratic government government that is elected by popular vote.

diplomacy peaceful negotiation between two or more states.

draft system in the USA, the term for conscription.

dysentery an infection of the intestine which occurs in areas with poor standards of hygiene.

firing squad a group of soldiers whose job is to execute those sentenced to death by shooting.

fraternization association on friendly terms between two people or groups of people.

military service service in one of the armed forces.

mobilization the act of preparing for war.

munitions military equipment.

mutiny rebellion against higher command.

nationalist someone who is passionately loyal to his or her own country.

pacifist someone who believes in finding a negotiated settlement rather than resorting to violence and war.

periscope a device that uses mirrors to allow someone to see objects that are not in their direct line of vision, for example over the top of a trench.

reconnaissance the act of obtaining vital information about enemy movements and positions.

reparations compensation.

reservists someone who serves in the reserve regiments of a nation's armed forces.

salient a 'bulge' into enemy territory of the front line of an attacking force.

sniper a marksman who fires at individual enemy soldiers.

stalemate a situation in conflict where neither side can make a move.

Territorials members of the Territorial Army, the reserve force of the British Army.

trajectory the path taken by an object moving through the air.

trench fever an infectious fever caused by the bites of lice.

war of attrition a tactic whereby one side hopes to wear its enemy down by inflicting more casualties than the enemy can inflict on it.

Further information

FURTHER READING

Christine Hatt, *Evans History in Writing: The First World War*, Evans Brothers, 2000

Jennifer D. Keene, *Seminar Studies in History: The United States and the First World War*, Longman, 2000

Frank McDonough, *Cambridge Perspectives in History: The Origins of the First and Second World Wars*, Cambridge University Press, 1997

Stuart Robson, *Seminar Studies in History: The First World War*, Longman, 1998

OTHER SOURCES

Malcolm Brown, *The Imperial War Museum Book of The First World War*, Sidgwick and Jackson/IWM, 1991

Malcolm Brown, *The Imperial War Museum Book of The Somme*, Sidgwick and Jackson/IWM, 1996

Malcolm Brown, *The Imperial War Museum Book of the Western Front*, Sidgwick and Jackson/IWM, 1994

Martin J. Farrar, *News from the Front*, Sutton Publishing, 1999

Niall Ferguson, *The Pity of War*, Penguin, 1998

Richard Holmes, *The Western Front*, BBC Books, 2001

John Keegan, *The First World War*, Hutchinson, 2001

John Laffin, *British Butchers and Bunglers of World War One*, Bramley Books, 1998

Lyn Macdonald, *1914-1918 Voices and Images of the Great War*, Penguin 1991

Lyn Macdonald, *To the Last Man*, Penguin, 1999

John Mosier, *The Myth of the Great War*, Profile Books, 2002

Colin Nicolson, *The Longman Campanion to the First World War Europe 1914-1918*, Longman, 2001

A.J.P. Taylor, *The First World War*, Penguin, 1970

PLACES TO VISIT

Imperial War Museum
Lambeth Road, London SE1 6HZ
Tel: 020 7416 5000

Imperial War Museum Duxford
The Airfield, Cambridge, Cambridgeshire, CB2 4QR
Tel: 01223 835000

NOTE ON SOURCES

A source is information about the past. Sources can take many forms, from books, films and documents to physical objects and sound recordings.

Essentially there are two types of source, primary and secondary. Primary sources date from around the time you are studying; secondary sources, such as books like this, have been produced since that time. In general, primary sources are more immediate but contain much narrower information than secondary sources. Moreover, primary sources need handling with care.

Here are some guidelines to bear in mind when approaching a written or drawn primary source:

1. Who produced it (a politician, cartoonist, etc.?) and why? What was their motive? Were they trying to make a point?
2. When exactly was the source produced? What was going on at the time? Detail is key here, not just the year but sometimes even down to the exact time of day.
3. Might the source have been altered by an editor, censor, translator? (Possible change in translation is very important.)
4. Where was the source produced? Which country, town, region, etc?
5. Does the source tie in with other sources you have met, primary and secondary, or does it offer a new point of view?
6. Where has the source come from? Has it been selected by someone else (probably to prove a point – beware!) or did you find it through your own researches? Basically, the only really valid primary sources are those uncovered in genuine research – others are just playing at history.

Index